10일투자 냉(가슴)빵(뚫린) 영어

문귀남 박양우 공저

백산출판사

10일투자, 냉(가슴) 뻥(뚫린) 영어

To our God, family, friends, and those who will benefit from this book!

머리말

이 책은 외국인을 만날 때 '울렁증'으로 고생하는 초보적인 영어회화에 관심 있는 학생과 일반인들을 대상으로 만들어졌다.

외국인을 처음 만났을 때 나누는 생활영어를 비롯하여 해외 여행시 필요한 기본적인 비행기표 예약, 세관통과, 호텔객실 예약 등과 같은 상황별 대화와 식당영어 그리고 쇼핑에 필요한 간단한 영어회화를 위주로 편집되었다.

하루에 한 unit씩 10일만 투자해도 답답한 가슴이 뻥 뚫리도록 되어 있다. 또한 각 unit별로 그날 배운 내용과 본인의 회화실력을 연습문제를 통해 꾸준하게 체크해볼 수 있도록 구성했다.

부록에서는 영어학습에 있어서 꼭 필요한 인칭대명사, 불규칙 동사와 시사영어, 그리고 기수와 서수, 방향, 신체 부위명, 가족관계, 요일, 월, 사계절, 시점의 분류, 방향과 장소의 전치사 및 부사, 동물이름, 스포츠 게임, 가벼운 병명, 빈도부사, 옷 사이즈, 과일종류, 색깔, 보석류와 액세서리 같은 기초회화에 필요한 기본적이고 필수적인 내용들을 실어 학습자들의 영어실력 향상에 만전을 기했다.

아무쪼록 이 한 권의 영어교재를 통해서 학습자들의 꽉 막힌 가슴이 속시원히 뻥 뚫리기를 간절히 기원한다.

2009년 11월 연구실에서

문귀남 · 박양우 교수 씀

CONTENTS

UNIT 1

Greetings 1

왕10일투자,

냉(가슴)뻥(뚫린)영어

Unit 1

Greetings 1

YAEJIN : Hello, nice to meet you.
= glad,
= pleased,
= happy,
= it's a pleasure
만나서 반갑습니다.

DANIEL : Nice to meet you, too.
저도요.

YAEJIN : I'm Yaejin. What's your name?
전 예진입니다. 성함이 어떻게 됩니까?

DANIEL : My name is Daniel Mun. But please call me Daniel.
제 이름은 문 다니엘입니다. 다니엘이라고 불러주세요.

설명 서양인들은 친하게 지내고 싶은 사람들에게 자신들의 성이 아닌 이름(first name)을 불러달라고 부탁함.

YAEJIN : Okay, Daniel.

By the way, how do you spell your first name?

알았어요, 다니엘.

그런데, 이름 스펠링은 어떻게 쓰세요?

설명 이름은 first name, 혹은 given name이라고 하며, 성은 last name, family name, 또는 surname이라고 한다. 한국인에게는 미국사람과 달리 중간 이름인 middle name이 없음.

DANIEL : It's D-A-N-I-E-L.

D-A-N-I-E-L 입니다.

YAEJIN : Where are you from, Daniel?

= Where is your hometown, Daniel?

= Where do you come from, Daniel?

다니엘 고향은 어디에요?

DANIEL : I'm from Canada.

전 캐나다에서 왔습니다.

YAEJIN : So, you're Canadian.

What is the capital city of Canada?

그러면 당신은 캐나다인이군요.

캐나다의 수도는 어디죠?

DANIEL : It's Ottawa.

오타와입니다.

YAEJIN : Where in Canada are you from?
= What part of Canada
당신은 캐나다 어디 출신입니까?

DANIEL : I'm from Toronto.
토론토 출신입니다.

YAEJIN : That's a great city.
What do you do for a living?
토론토는 아주 좋은 도시죠.
직업은 뭐에요?

설명 '직업이 무엇입니까?'란 표현은 What's your occupation?, What's your job?, What's your profession?, What do you do? 등 다양함.

DANIEL : I'm a university student, and I have a part-time job, too.
≠ full-time
전 대학생입니다. 그리고 아르바이트도 하고요.

설명 아르바이트(arbeit)는 영어가 아닌 독일어임.

YAEJIN : Oh, really?
Where do you go to school?
= Which university do you go to?
오, 그래요?
어느 학교에 다녀요?

DANIEL : I go to the University of Toronto.
전 토론토 대학교에 다닙니다.

YAEJIN : Really! I know it's one of the most prestigious universities
= famous
in the world. What year are you in?
= What grade are you in?
정말요! 토론토 대학교는 세계 명문대학중의 하나로 알고 있습니다. 몇 학년이세요?

DANIEL : I'm in my second year. Sophomore.
전 2학년입니다.

설명 미국대학에서는 1학년은 Freshman, 2학년은 Sophomore, 3학년은 Junior, 그리고 4학년은 Senior이라고 함.

YAEJIN : What's your major (or minor)?
= What do you major (or minor) in?
전공(부전공)은 뭐에요?

설명 복수 전공은 double major라고 함.

DANIEL : My major is English Education.
= I major in English Education.
= I specialize in
전 영어교육학을 전공하고 있습니다.

YAEJIN : That sounds interesting!

Do you like your major?

= How do you like your major?

아주 재미있겠네요.

전공은 마음에 드세요?

DANIEL : I love it very much.

English is my favorite subject.

= best

아주 마음에 듭니다.

영어는 제가 가장 좋아하는 과목이거든요.

Exercise 1

Translate the following questions into English.

1. 만나서 반갑습니다.

2. Daniel이라고 불러 주세요.

3. 이름 스펠링이 어떻게 됩니까?

4. 고향이 어디입니까?

5. 캐나다의 수도는 어디입니까?

6. 당신은 캐나다 어디 출신입니까?

7. 직업이 무엇입니까?

8. 어느 학교에 다닙니까?

9. 몇 학년입니까?

10. 전공(부전공)이 무엇입니까?

11. 전공이 마음에 듭니까?

UNIT 2

Greetings 2

오10일투자,

냉(가슴)뻥(뚫린)영어

Unit 2

Greetings 2

YAEJIN : Where do you live in Korea, Daniel?
다니엘, 한국 어디에 살아요?

DANIEL : I live in Yatap, Bundang.
What about you Yaejin?
= How about
전 분당 야탑에 살아요.
예진씨는요?

YAEJIN : I live in Gangnam, Seoul.
전 서울 강남에 살아요.

DANIEL : That's a nice place.
좋은데 사시네요

YAEJIN : I'm sorry but when is your birthday?
= when were you born?
죄송하지만 생일이 언제에요?

DANIEL : My birthday is December 15th.
제 생일은 12월 15일이에요.

YAEJIN : How do you go to school everyday?
매일 학교는 어떻게 다녀요?

DANIEL : I commute by subway.
= go to school
지하철로 통학해요.

YAEJIN : How long does it take?
얼마나 걸려요?

DANIEL : Oh, it takes about one & half hours from my home.
집에서 대충 1시간 반 정도 걸려요.

YAEJIN : Wow! It's a long way.
꽤 먼 거리네요.

DANIEL : Yes, it is.
그렇죠.

YAEJIN : What day is it today?
오늘이 무슨 요일인가요?

DANIEL : It's Monday.
월요일이에요.

YAEJIN : What's today's date?
오늘이 며칠이죠?

DANIEL : It's September 21st.
9월 21일이에요.

YAEJIN : Thank you, Daniel!
It was nice meeting you.
I look forward to meeting you again.
= really wish to meet
다니엘 고마워요.
만나서 반가웠어요.
다시 만나길 학수고대할게요.

DANIEL : I hope so, too. Good-bye.
저도 그러길 바래요. 안녕히 가세요.

Exercise 2

Translate the following questions into English.

1. 한국 어디에서 사십니까?

2. 죄송하지만 생일이 언제입니까?

3. 학교는 어떻게 다닙니까?

4. 얼마나 걸립니까?

5. 오늘이 무슨 요일입니까?

6. 오늘이 며칠입니까?

7. 만나서 반가웠습니다.

8. 또 만나 뵙기를 고대합니다.

9. 저도 그러길 바랍니다.

UNIT 3

Flight Reservation

오 10일투자,

냉(가슴)뻥(뚫린)영어

Unit 3

Flight Reservation

YAEJIN : Korean Air. May I help you?
= Can I help you?
= Is there anything I can do for you?
= What can I do for you?
대한항공입니다. 도와드릴까요?

DANIEL : Yes, please. I'd like to book a ticket to Toronto, Canada.
≠ No, thank you. = reserve
네. 캐나다 토론토로 가는 표를 예약하고 싶습니다.

YAEJIN : Okay. May I have your name, please?
= What's your name?
= Would you tell me your name?
네. 성함이 어떻게 되세요?

DANIEL : It's Daniel Mun.
문 다니엘입니다.

YAEJIN : Okay. When do you plan to go?
= leave,
= depart

네. 언제 떠나실 예정입니까?

DANIEL : This Sunday. That's 17th.

이번 일요일에요. 17일.

YAEJIN : OK. And how long do you want to stay in Toronto?
= how many days

알겠습니다. 토론토에는 얼마동안 체류하기를 원하세요?

DANIEL : About a week.

약 1주일정도요.

YAEJIN : So, you want to return to Seoul, on the 23rd, next Saturday.
= come back

그렇다면 다음 주 토요일인 23일에 귀국하신다는 말씀이군요.

DANIEL : That's right.
= That's correct.

그렇습니다.

YAEJIN : Do you want a one-way or round trip ticket?

편도를 원하세요, 아니면 왕복표를 원하세요?

DANIEL : One round trip ticket, please.
How much is a round trip ticket?
왕복표를 주세요.
왕복표는 얼마에요?

YAEJIN : It's 1,700,000 won including tax at this peak season.
≠ excluding ≠ off season
Would that be OK?
지금 같은 성수기에는 세금포함해서 170만원 입니다.
괜찮으세요?

DANIEL : That's fine.
Do you accept credit cards?
= take
좋습니다.
신용카드 받으세요?

YAEJIN : Certainly! Now your seat's reserved.
Of course! = booked.
Sure!
Please come to the airport at least two hours prior to your departure time. = before
≠ arrival
물론입니다. 이제 손님 좌석은 예약이 되었습니다.
출발시각 두 시간 전에 공항으로 나와 주세요.

DANIEL : Okay. Thank you very much!
그럴게요. 대단히 감사합니다.

YAEJIN : Thank you! Have a nice day!
= good,
= wonderful,
= terrific
감사합니다. 좋은 하루 되십시오.

Exercise 3

Translate the following questions into English.

1. 대한항공입니다. 무엇을 도와 드릴까요?

2. 토론토로 가는 비행기표를 예약하고 싶습니다.

3. 성함이 어떻게 되세요?

4. 언제 떠날 예정입니까?

5. 토론토에는 얼마동안 체류할 예정입니까?

6. 편도표를 원하세요, 아니면 왕복표를 원하세요?

7. 왕복표는 얼마입니까?

8. 신용카드 받으세요?

9. 공항에는 적어도 출발 두 시간 전에는 나와 주세요.

10. 즐거운 하루 보내세요.

UNIT 4

At the Customs Office

오10일투자,

냉(가슴) 뻥(뚫린) 영어

Unit 4

At the Customs Office

DANIEL : Hello.

May I see your passport and customs declaration form please?

설명 declare는 신고하다의 뜻으로 공항에서 자주 쓰임. Do you have anything to declare? 신고할 것이 있습니까? No, nothing. 아무것도 없습니다. = make due statement of goods for duty or tax

안녕하세요.

여권과 세관신고서를 보여주시겠습니까?

설명 출국카드는 embarkation card, 혹은 departure card 그리고 입국카드는 disembarkation card , 혹은 arrival card라고 함.

YAEJIN : Here you are!

여기 있습니다!

설명 물건을 상대방에게 건네줄 때는 Here you are!, Here we are! 등을 쓰며 찾는 물건을 가리킬 때는 Here it is!를 사용함.

DANIEL : What is the purpose of your visit?

= nature　　= trip

= reason

방문목적이 무엇입니까?

YAEJIN : I'm here on business.

= for pleasure

= for sightseeing

= for my honeymoon trip

여기에 출장차 왔습니다.

= 놀러

= 관광차

= 신혼 여행차

DANIEL : What do you do?

= What do you do for a living?

= What's your occupation?

= What's your job?

= What's your profession?

직업이 무엇입니까?

YAEJIN : I'm a professor.

I'm with LG.

I work at Samsung Electronics.

I work for Harvard University as a professor.

교수입니다.

LG에 근무합니다.
삼성전자에 근무합니다.
하버드대학교 교수로 재직 중입니다.

설명 ~에 근무하다는 표현으로는 be+with, work at, work for 등으로 사용한다.

DANIEL : I see. How long do you plan to stay?
= How long are you going to stay?
= will you
알겠습니다. 얼마동안 체류할 계획입니까?

설명 I see(알겠다)는 몰랐던 사실을 알게 되었을 때, 그리고 I know(알고 있다)는 이미 알고 있던 사실을 또 듣게 될 때 사용됨.

YAEJIN : Oh. About a week
two weeks.
three months.
약 1주간요.
약 2주간요.
약 3개월간요.

DANIEL : Thank you. You may go.
= Thanks a lot. You can go.
감사합니다. 가셔도 좋습니다.

Exercise 4

Translate the following questions into English.

1. 여권과 세관신고서를 보여 주시겠습니까?

2. 여기 있습니다.

3. 방문목적이 무엇입니까?

4. 관광차 왔습니다.

5. 뭐 하시는 분이세요?

6. 저는 Harvard University 교수입니다.

7. 얼마동안 머무실 계획입니까?

8. 이제 가셔도 좋습니다.

UNIT 5

At a Hotel

오10일투자,

냉(가슴) 뻥(뚫린) 영어

Unit 5

At a Hotel

YAEJIN : Good evening, sir. Do you have a reservation?

= Did you make a reservation?

안녕하세요. 예약하셨습니까?

DANIEL : Yes, I do.

네.

YAEJIN : May I have your name, please?

성함이 어떻게 되세요?

DANIEL : Daniel Mun.

문 다니엘입니다.

YAEJIN : Just one moment, please······ That's for five nights, Mr.

= Wait a minute

= Wait a second

Mun?

잠깐만요······ 5박이죠 문선생님?

DANIEL : Yes, that's correct. Five nights.
= right
네, 맞습니다. 5박6일입니다.

설명 일반적으로 호텔에서 몇 박 며칠이라고 말할 때 몇 박만 이야기하고 며칠은 말하지 않음.

YAEJIN : Will you pay by credit card or cash?
(Visa, Master Card, American Express Card, Diner's Card, etc.)
신용카드로 결제하시겠어요? 아니면 현금으로?

DANIEL : Credit card.
신용카드로 할게요.

YAEJIN : May I have your credit card, please?
신용카드 주시겠습니까?

DANIEL : Certainly. Here you are.
What time is your check-out time?
≠ check-in
물론이죠. 여기 있습니다.
몇 시가 퇴실시간입니까?

YAEJIN : It's by noon.
Please sign here.
= Would you put your signature here, please?
정오까지입니다.

여기에 서명해 주세요.

DANIEL : Okay.

네.

YAEJIN : The bellman will take you to your room.

≠ bring

(cf. carry-on-bag = 손가방)

Is that your luggage?

= baggage?

벨맨이 손님방으로 안내할거에요.

저건 손님 짐 가방인가요?

DANIEL : Yes, it is. Thank you.

네, 그렇습니다. 고마워요.

YAEJIN : Thank you, sir. Have a nice day!

≠ ma'am = Enjoy your stay!

감사합니다. 즐거운 하루 되십시오.

설명 호텔방의 종류

single,	twin,	double,	queen,	king,	suite room
싱글	트윈	더블	퀸사이즈	킹사이즈	스위트 룸

Exercise 5

Translate the following questions into English.

1. 예약이 되어 있습니까?

2. 계산은 신용카드로 하시겠어요? 아니면 현금으로 하시겠어요?

3. 신용카드 좀 보여 주시겠습니까?

4. 퇴실시간이 언제입니까?

5. 여기에 사인해 주시겠습니까?

6. 저게 당신 짐 가방입니까?

UNIT 6

At a Restaurant 1

오10일투자,

냉(가슴)뻥(뚫린)영어

Unit 6

At a Restaurant 1

DANIEL : Hello. May I help you?

안녕하세요. 도와드릴까요?

YAEJIN : Yes, can I get a table?

= do you have a table available?

네. 자리 하나 있습니까?

DANIEL : Sure. How many in your party?

= For how many people?

물론이죠. 몇 분이세요?

YAEJIN : Just myself.

= me

단지 저 혼자입니다.

DANIEL : Okay. Follow me, please.

= Come with me

And here's your menu. I'll be back in a few seconds.

Would you like a drink before your meal?
알겠습니다. 저를 따라오세요.
그리고 여기에 메뉴판이 있습니다. 잠시 후 다시 오겠습니다.
식사 전에 음료수라도 하시겠습니까?

설명 식사라는 뜻을 가진 meal은 breakfast, lunch, or dinner를 포함함.
= supper

설명 서양에서는 식사를 주문하기 전에 간단한 음료수나 술을 먼저 시키는 경향이 있음.

YAEJIN : Yes. A glass of coke, please.
= coca-cola
네. 콜라 한 잔주세요.

DANIEL : Okay. I'll be right back.
Here's your coke!
Are you ready to order, sir?
= Would you like to order,
= May I take your order,
알겠습니다. 금방 다녀오겠습니다.
콜라 여기 있습니다.
주문하시겠습니까?

YAEJIN : Not really. I don't really know what to order.
What would you recommend for me?
글쎄요. 뭘 주문해야 할지 잘 모르겠네요.

뭘 추천하시겠습니까?

DANIEL : How about a New York steak?

Have you ever tried it before?

= eaten

= tasted

뉴욕스테이크는 어떠세요?

드셔본 적이 있으십니까?

설명 how about, what about은 ~은 어떻습니까의 뜻임.

YAEJIN : No, never.

= not even once.

아뇨. 한 번도 없어요.

DANIEL : It's today's special and very delicious.

= tasty

= good

그게 저희식당에서 오늘의 특별메뉴인데 아주 맛있어요.

YAEJIN : OK, then.

I'll have the New York steak.

= try

= eat

그럼 알겠어요.

뉴욕스테이크를 먹어볼게요.

DANIEL : How would you like that cooked?

= How would you like it?

= How do you want it done?

어떻게 구워드릴까요?

YAEJIN : Well-done, please.

Medium,

Rare,

잘 익혀서 주세요.

적당하게 익혀서 주세요.

설익혀서 주세요.

DANIEL : OK. That's one well-done steak.

Would you like soup or salad?

알겠습니다. 잘 익힌 스테이크 1인분 입니다.

스프를 원하세요? 아니면 샐러드를 원하세요?

YAEJIN : Salad, please.

샐러드로 주세요.

Exercise 6

Translate the following questions into English.

1. 자리 하나 있습니까?

2. 몇 분이세요?

3. 저를 따라 오십시오.

4. 식사 전에 음료수를 하시겠습니까?

5. 금방 오겠습니다.

6. 주문하시겠습니까?

7. 뭘 주문해야 할지 모르겠습니다.

8. 뭘 추천해 주시겠습니까?

9. 뉴욕 스테이크 어떻습니까? 한번 드셔 본적이 있습니까?

10. 스테이크는 어떻게 구워 드릴까요?

UNIT 7

At a Restaurant 2

오 10일 투자,

냉(가슴) 뻥(뚫린) 영어

Unit 7

At a Restaurant 2

DANIEL : What dressing would you like?

= sauce

드레싱은 어떤 걸로 원하세요?

YAEJIN : What kind of dressing do you have?

드레싱종류는 어떤 게 있습니까?

DANIEL : We have Italian, French, and Thousand Island.

이탈리언, 프렌치, 그리고 사우전 아이랜드가 있습니다.

YAEJIN : I'll try the French dressing, please.

전 프렌치드레싱으로 하겠습니다.

DANIEL : Okay. I'll be right back.

알겠습니다. 금방 돌아올게요.

DANIEL : Here's your steak. Enjoy the meal!

여기 주문하신 스테이크 나왔습니다. 맛있게 드십시오.

YAEJIN : Thank you.
고맙습니다.

DANIEL : Did you enjoy the meal?
식사 잘 하셨습니까?

YAEJIN : Yes, I did.
네. 잘 했습니다.

DANIEL : How did it taste?
= How was it?
= Was it delicious?
맛이 어땠습니까?

YAEJIN : It was very delicious.
≠ tasteless
≠ bland
≠ terrible
≠ awful
매우 맛있었어요.
맛이 없었어요.
맛이 싱거웠어요.
맛이 엉망이었어요.
맛이 형편없었어요.

DANIEL : Would you like some dessert?
(cf. desert = an arid, sandy region, 사막)
후식을 좀 하시겠습니까?

YAEJIN : No, thank you. I'm full already.
= satisfied
고맙지만 사양하겠습니다. 벌써 배불러요.
May I have the check, please?
= bill
계산서 갖다 주시겠습니까?

설명 영수증은 receipt 이라고 함.

DANIEL : Here you are.
여기 있습니다.

YAEJIN : How much do I owe you?
= How much is it?
계산이 얼마´ 입니까?

DANIEL : You owe me $27 including tax.
≠ excluding
세금 포함해서 27달러입니다.

YAEJIN : Here's $30.
Keep the change as your tip.
= Take

여기 30달러입니다.
잔돈은 팁으로 가지세요.

DANIEL : Thanks a lot. Have a nice day.
= Thank you very much.
대단히 감사합니다. 즐거운 하루 되십시오.

YAEJIN : Thanks. Take care(of yourself)!
= Take it easy!
= Good-bye!
감사합니다. 조심해가세요.

Exercise 7

Translate the following questions into English.

1. 어떤 소스(드레싱)를 좋아 하세요?

2. 소스 종류가 어떤 게 있습니까?

3. 프렌치 드레싱을 한번 먹어보죠.

4. 식사 맛있게 하세요.

5. 식사 잘 하셨습니까?

6. 맛이 어땠습니까?

7. 매우 맛있었습니다.

8. 후식을 하시겠습니까?

9. 괜찮습니다. 전 지금 배부릅니다.

10. 계산서 갖다 주시겠습니까?

11. 제가 얼마 드리면 되죠?

12. 잔돈은 팁으로 가지세요.

UNIT 8

Asking for Directions

오10일투자,

냉(가슴)뻥(뚫린)영어

Unit 8

Asking for Directions

YAEJIN : Excuse me! I need some directions.

실례합니다. 길 안내가 좀 필요합니다.

DANIEL : Sure. What do you want to know?

그러죠. 알고 싶은 게 뭐죠?

YAEJIN : Well, I'd like to do some sightseeing today.

= I'd like to visit some tourist attractions

= I'd like to visit some famous tourist places

글쎄요. 오늘은 관광을 좀 하고 싶습니다.

DANIEL : All right(= Okay).

I think you should see the CN Tower and Niagara Falls.

= In my opinion = visit

좋습니다.

제 생각에는 CN 타워와 나이아가라 폭포를 보셔야 될 것 같은데요.

YAEJIN : What's so good about the CN Tower and Niagara Falls?
CN 타워와 나이아가라 폭포가 뭐가 그렇게 좋은가요?

DANIEL : Well, the CN Tower is the tallest building in the world.
= highest
그게, CN 타워는 세계에서 가장 높은 빌딩입니다.

YAEJIN : How tall is it?
= high
얼마나 높은데요?

DANIEL : It's 553m.
It has a spectacular and breathtaking view.
= impressive = thrillingly beautiful
높이가 553m이며 아주 숨 막힐 정도로 장관입니다.

YAEJIN : Really. Now I feel like seeing the tower for sure.
= really wish to see
= really want to see
When was it built?
= How old is the building?
그래요? 이제 정말로 그 타워를 보고싶다는 느낌이 드네요.
언제 건축되었나요?

DANIEL : It was built in 1976.
CN타워는 1976년에 건축되었죠.

YAEJIN : I see. What's the best way to get there?

= What is the easiest way to get there?

= How can I get there?

= Could you tell me the way to the CN Tower?

= Would you show me the way to the CN Tower?

= Please direct me to the CN Tower.

알겠습니다. 그곳에 가는 가장 빠른 길을 알려주시겠습니까?

DANIEL : Well, the CN Tower is just around the corner.

= very close

You go out of the hotel, turn right and it's a two-minute walk.

You can't miss it.

= You will find it easily.

CN타워는 바로 코너만 돌면 있어요.

호텔에서 나가셔서, 오른쪽으로 도시면 2분 정도 거리에 있습니다.

바로 찾으실 겁니다.

YAEJIN : I see. What about the Niagara Falls?

알겠습니다. 나이아가라폭포는 어떻게 되죠?

DANIEL : If you go by car, it takes about one hour from here, if there's no traffic jam.

= heavy traffic

= traffic congestion

만약에 차로 가시면 교통체증만 없다면 여기에서부터 약 1 시간정도 걸립니다.

YAEJIN : OK, thanks a lot. Oh, one more thing.

Where is the nearest bank around here?

= closest

I need to withdraw some money.

≠ deposit

DANIEL : There's one ATM just across from this hotel.

= Automatic/Automated-Teller Machine

이 호텔 바로 맞은편에 자동인출기가 있습니다.

YAEJIN : Thank you very much.

대단히 감사합니다.

DANIEL : You're very welcome.

천만에요.

Exercise 8

Translate the following questions into English.

1. 실례합니다. 길안내가 좀 필요합니다.

2. 무엇을 알고 싶으세요?

3. 오늘 관광을 좀 하고 싶습니다.

4. CN Tower와 나이아가라 폭포가 뭐가 그렇게 좋은가요?

5. CN Tower의 높이는 얼마나 됩니까?

6. CN Tower는 언제 건축되었습니까?

7. CN Tower로 가는 가장 빠른 길은 무엇입니까?

8. 여기에서 가장 가까운 은행은 어디에 있습니까?

9. 저는 돈을 좀 뽑아야 합니다.

10. 이 호텔 건너편에 자동인출기가 있습니다.

UNIT 9

Rent a Car

오10일투자,

냉(가슴)뻥(뚫린)영어

Unit 9

Rent a Car

DANIEL : May I help you?
도와 드릴까요?

YAEJIN : Yes, I'd like to rent a car.
= want to
네. 차를 한 대 대여하고 싶습니다.

DANIEL : What kind of car would you like?
We have compact, mid-sized, and full-sized cars.
어떤 차를 원하세요?
저희는 소형, 중형, 그리고 대형차가 있습니다.

YAEJIN : How many seats does the compact sized car have?
소형차는 좌석이 얼마나 됩니까?

DANIEL : It has four seats, but the back seat is rather small.
≠ front seat
좌석이 4개입니다. 그리고 뒷좌석은 다소 좁습니다.

YAEJIN : Which car would you recommend for me?
저한테는 어떤 차를 추천하시겠습니까?

DANIEL : If you want an enjoyable ride,
I would suggest a comfortable mid-sized car.
= recommend ≠ uncomfortable
즐거운 운전을 하고 싶으시다면,
저는 편안한 중형차를 추천하고 싶은데요.

YAEJIN : OK. What is the rate for the mid-sized car a day?
= per day?
좋습니다. 중형차는 하루에 얼마입니까?

DANIEL : $30 per day without tax for a Camry.
≠ with
캠리는 세금을 제외하고 하루에 30달러입니다.

YAEJIN : That sounds good. I'll take it.
= rent it.
괜찮네요. 그것으로 하지요.

DANIEL : How long do you want to rent it for?
얼마동안 대여하기를 원하세요?

YAEJIN : Just for one day.
단 하루요.

DANIEL : All right. May I see your (international) driver's license and a credit card, please?
좋습니다. (국제) 운전 면허증과 신용카드를 보여주시겠습니까?

YAEJIN : Here you are.
여기 있습니다.

DANIEL : Okay. Would you put your signature right here?
네. 여기에 서명해 주시겠습니까?

YAEJIN : Sure. How about mileage and gas?
= gasoline
물론이죠. 마일리지와 기름은 어떻게 됩니까?

DANIEL : No charge for mileage and gas.
Just fill up the gas when you return the car.
= bring back
마일리지와 기름은 따로 계산하지는 않습니다.
그냥 차를 갖고 오실 때 기름만 채워주세요.

YAEJIN : By what time should I return the car?
몇 시까지 차를 갖고 와야 되죠?

DANIEL : By noon tomorrow.
≠ midnight
내일 정오까지입니다.

YAEJIN : I see.

알겠습니다.

DANIEL : Take this key and your car is right outside this building. Enjoy your ride! And drive carefully!

이 열쇠를 가져가세요. 차는 바로 이 건물 밖에 있습니다. 잘 타세요. 그리고 운전 조심하세요.

YAEJIN : Thanks a lot. See you tomorrow.

대단히 감사합니다. 내일 뵙겠습니다.

Exercise 9

Translate the following questions into English.

1. 차를 한 대 대여 하고 싶습니다.

2. 어떤 종류의 차를 원하십니까?

3. 중형차는 하루에 얼마입니까?

4. 면허증과 신용카드를 보여 주시겠습니까?

5. 마일리지와 기름은 어떻게 합니까?

6. 차를 갖고 오실 때 기름만 가득 채워 오세요.

7. 몇 시까지 차를 가져와야 합니까?

8. 내일 정오까지 입니다.

9. 운전 잘 하세요. 그리고 운전 조심하세요.

UNIT 10

Shopping

오10일투자,

냉(가슴)뻥(뚫린)영어

Unit 10

Shopping

DANIEL : May I help you?

도와 드릴까요?

YAEJIN : Yes, please.

I'd like to get a diamond ring for my husband.

네, 부탁합니다.

제 남편에게 줄 다이아몬드 반지를 사고 싶습니다.

DANIEL : How much do you want to spend?

= What is your budget?

얼마정도 쓰기를 원하세요?

YAEJIN : Around two thousand dollars.

= About

= Approximately

대략 2천 달러 정도요.

DANIEL : OK. Come this way, please.
These are one-karat diamonds.
그렇습니까. 이쪽으로 오시죠.
이 반지들은 일 캐럿 다이아몬드입니다.

YAEJIN : How much is this?
이건 얼마입니까?

DANIEL : The regular price is $2,500, but this week it's on sale.
= able to be bought at a reduced price
So it's only $1,999.
정가는 2,500달러입니다. 하지만 이번 주에는 할인판매하고 있습니다.
그래서 1,999달러에 판매합니다.

설명 on sale은 염가판매, for sale (= available for purchase)은 판매용이라는 뜻이며, not for sale은 비매품이란 뜻임.

YAEJIN : Can't you give me any additional discounts?
Otherwise I might have to shop around.
= If not, = visit other places
추가 할인은 안 되겠습니까?
안되면 다른 가게를 둘러봐야 할 것 같은데요.

DANIEL : I'm sorry. This is the bottom price.
= lowest

We guarantee the lowest price in town.

Besides, you don't have to pay any sales tax here.

= More over,

= In addition

죄송하지만 이게 최저 가격입니다.

저희 가게는 이 도시에서는 최저가를 보장하고 있습니다.

게다가, 손님은 여기에서 판매세를 낼 필요가 없습니다.

YAEJIN : Oh, really? I'll take it, then.

Could you wrap it for me?

그래요? 그렇다면 사지요.

포장해 주시겠습니까?

DANIEL : Sure. How are you going to pay?

Cash or charge?

= credit card?

물론이죠. 계산은 어떻게 하시겠습니까?

현금이에요 아니면 카드로?

YAEJIN : Charge it to my Visa card, please.

= Place the price

제 비자카드로 결제해 주세요.

DANIEL : May I see your card, please?

카드를 보여 주시겠습니까?

YAEJIN : Here you are.
여기 있습니다.

DANIEL : Would you sign here, please?
여기에 서명해 주시겠습니까?

YAEJIN : Sure.
그럼요.

DANIEL : Thank you very much.
Have a good day!
대단히 감사합니다.
즐거운 하루 되십시오.

YAEJIN : Thank you. Good-bye!
고맙습니다. 안녕히 계세요.

Exercise 10

Translate the following questions into English.

1. 예산은 얼마 정도로 잡고 있습니까?

2. 좀더 깎아 주시면 안되겠습니까?

3. 이 가격이 최저가격입니다.

4. 그리고 여기서는 판매세를 내실 필요가 없습니다.

5. 그것을 포장해 주시겠습니까?

6. 현금으로 지불하시겠어요, 아니면 카드로 하시겠어요?

7. 제 카드로 결재해 주세요.

Answers for Exercise

오 10 일투자,

냉(가슴)뻥(뚫린) 영어

Answers for Exercise 1

1. Hello, <u>nice</u> to meet you.

   = <u>glad,</u>

   = <u>pleased,</u>

   = <u>happy</u>

2. Please call me Daniel.

3. How do you spell your first(= given) name?

4. <u>Where are you from?</u>

= <u>Where is your hometown?</u>

= <u>Where do you come from?</u>

5. What is the capital city of Canada?

6. <u>Where in Canada</u> are you from?

= <u>What part of Canada</u>

7. <u>What do you do for a living?</u>

= <u>What do you do?</u>

= <u>What's your occupation?</u>

= <u>What's your profession?</u>

= <u>What's your job?</u>

8. Where do you go to school?

= Which university (or school) do you go to?

9. What year are you in?

= What grade are you in?

10. What's your major (or minor)?

= What do you major (or minor) in?

11. Do you like your major?

= How do you like your major?

Answers for Exercise 2

1. Where do you live in Korea?
2. I'm sorry but when is your birthday?

   = when were you born?
3. How do you go to school everyday?
4. How long does it take?
5. What day is it today?
6. What's today's date?
7. It was nice meeting you.
8. I hope so, too.

Answers for Exercise 3

Dr. Mun's Magic Travel & Tourism English

1. Korean Air. May I help you?

   = Can I help you?

   = Is there anything I can do for you?

   = What can I do for you?

2. I'd like to book a ticket to Toronto, Canada.

   = reserve

3. May I have your name please?

   = What's your name?

   = Would you tell me your name?

4. When do you plan to go?

   = leave,

   = depart

5. How long do you want to stay in Toronto?

   = How many days

6. Do you want a one-way or round trip ticket?

7. How much is the round trip ticket?

8. Do you accept a credit card?

   = take

9. Please come to the airport at least two hours prior to your departure time. = before

10. Have a nice day!

= good

= wonderful

= terrific

Answers for Exercise 4

1. May I see your passport and customs declaration form please?
2. Here you are!
3. What is the purpose of your visit?

   = nature = trip

4. I'm here for sightseeing.
5. What do you do?

= What do you do for a living?

= What's your occupation?

= What's your job?

= What's your profession?

6. I work for Harvard University as a professor.

7. How long do you plan to stay?

= How long are you going to stay?

= will you

8. You may go now.

= You can go now.

Answers for Exercise 5

Dr. Mun's Magic Travel & Tourism English

1. Do you have a reservation?

= Did you make a reservation?

2. Will you pay by credit card or cash?

3. May I have your credit card, please?

4. What time is your check-out time?

5. Please sign here.

= Would you put your signature here, please?

6. Is that your luggage?

= baggage?

Answers for Exercise 6

Dr. Mun's Magic Travel & Tourism English

1. Can I get a table?

= Do you have a table available?

2. How many in your party?

= For how many people?

3. Follow me, please.

= Come with me

4. Would you like a drink before your meal?

5. I'll be right back.

6. Are you ready to order, sir?

= Would you like to order,

= May I take your order,

7. I don't really know what to order.

8. What would you recommend for me?

9. How about a New York steak? Have you ever tried it before?

= eaten

= tasted

10. How would you like your steak cooked?

= How would you like your steak?

= How do you want your steak done?

Answers for Exercise 7

1. What dressing would you like?

   = sauce

2. What kind of dressing do you have?
3. I'll try the French dressing, please.
4. Enjoy the meal!
5. Did you enjoy the meal?
6. How did it taste?

   = How was it?

   = Was it delicious?

7. It was very delicious.
8. Would you like some dessert?
9. No, thank you. I'm full already.

   = satisfied

10. May I have the <u>check</u>, please?

= <u>bill</u>

11. <u>How much do I owe you?</u>

= <u>How much is it?</u>

12. <u>Keep</u> the change as your tip.

= <u>Take</u>

Answers for Exercise 8

Dr. Mun's Magic Travel & Tourism English

1. Excuse me! I need some directions.
2. What do you want to know?
3. I'd like to <u>do some sightseeing</u> today.

= I'd like to <u>visit some tourist attractions</u>.

4. What's so good about the CN Tower and Niagara Falls?
5. How <u>tall</u> is the CN Tower?

= <u>high</u>

6. When was the CN Tower built?
7. <u>What's the best way to get to the CN Tower?</u>

= <u>How can I get to the CN Tower?</u>

= Could you tell me the way to the CN Tower?

= Would you show me the way to the CN Tower?

= Please direct me to the CN Tower.

8. Where is the nearest bank around here?

= closest

9. I need to withdraw some money.

10. There's one ATM just across from this hotel.

Answers for Exercise 9

Dr. Mun's Magic Travel & Tourism English

1. I'd like to rent a car.
2. What kind of car would you like?
3. What is the rate for the mid-sized car a day?

   = per day?

4. May I see your (international) driver's license and a credit card, please?
5. How about mileage and gas?

   = gasoline

6. Just fill up the gas when you return the car.

   = bring back

7. By what time should I return the car?

8. By noon tomorrow.

9. Enjoy your ride! And drive carefully.

Answers for Exercise 10

1. How much do you want to spend?

= What is your budget?

2. Can't you give me any additional discounts?

3. This is the bottom price.

= lowest

4. You don't have to pay any sales tax here.

5. Could you wrap it for me?

= Would

6. How are you going to pay? Cash or charge?

= Will you pay by credit card or cash?

7. Charge it to my Visa card, please.

각 Unit의
Words and Phrases 뜻풀이

오10일투자,

냉(가슴)뻥(뚫린)영어

각 Unit의 Words and Phrases 뜻풀이

Words and Phrases

v.: verb 동사		n.: noun 명사	
pron.: pronoun	대명사	prep.: preposition	전치사
adj.: adjective	형용사	adv.: adverb	부사
interj.: interjection	감탄사	conj.: conjunction	접속사

Unit 1

nice	adj. 즐거운, 기쁜, 멋진, 반가운
glad	adj. 기쁜, 반가운
pleased	adj. 기쁜, 기분 좋은, 반가운
happy	adj. 행복한, 기분 좋은
call	v. 전화하다, 부르다
by the way	(대화도중 화제를 바꿀 때)그건 그렇고
spell	v.~이라고 철자하다, 스펠링을 적다

hometown	n. 고향
Canadian	n. 캐나다인
	adj. 캐나다의, 캐나다인의
capital city	수도
Where in Canada ~?	캐나다 어디~?
What part of Canada ~?	캐나다 어느 지역~?
great	adj. 멋진, 위대한, 훌륭한
living	n. 생활
	adj. 살아 있는, 실재하는
part-time	adj. 비상근제인, 시간제의(보통 하루에 4시간 미만, 혹은 주말만 근무함)
	adv. 비상근제로, 시간제로
full-time	adj. 정규의, 상근의, 전임의
	adv. 상근제로, 전임으로
really	adv. 정말, 진짜로
most	adv. 가장, 최대의, 최고의
prestigious	adj. 명문의, 유명한
university	n. 대학교
year	n. 해, 년, 학년
grade	n. 학년, 점수, 등급
major	n. 전공
	adj. 주요한, 전공의
minor	n. 부전공, 미성년자
	adj. 중요하지 않은, 미성년의
major in	~을 전공하다
specialize in	~을 전공하다
sound	v. ~하게 들리다, 느껴지다, 생각 되다, 소리나다

	n. 소리, 음향, 음
	adj. 건전한,
favorite	adj. 가장 좋아하는, 가장 마음에 드는
	n. 가장 마음에 드는 사람 또는 물건
subject	n. 과목, 주제, 주어

Unit 2

What about ~?	~은 어떻습니까?
How about ~?	~은 어떻습니까?
place	n. 장소, 자리
	v. 두다, 놓다
birthday	n. 생일
born	adj. 태어난
commute	v. 통학하다, 통근하다
subway	n. 지하철
How long does it take?	얼마나 걸립니까?
wow	int. 와, 야
long way	먼 길, 먼 거리
day	n. 날, 일, 요일
date	n. 날짜
look forward to + (동)명사	~하기를 학수고대하다
hope	v. 희망하다, 바라다
	n. 희망, 소망
too	adv. ~도 또한, 역시, 너무, 매우

Unit 3

Yes, please!	예, 그렇게 해 주세요.
No, thank you.	고맙지만 사양하겠습니다.
would like to	~하고 싶습니다.
book	v. 예약하다, 표를 사다
	n. 책
reserve	v. 예약하다
plan	v. 계획하다
	n. 계획
leave	v. 떠나다
depart	v. 출발하다, 떠나다
stay	v. 체류하다, 머물다
	n. 체류
how many days ~?	며칠이나?
about	adv. 대략, 대충, 주위에
return	v. 돌아오다, 돌아가다, 돌려주다
	n. 귀환, 반환, 반납
next	adj. 다음의
That's right.	그렇습니다.
one-way	편도(의)
round trip	왕복여행
How much ~?	얼마~?
including	adj. ~을 포함해서
excluding	adj. ~을 포함하지 않고
peak season	성수기

off season	비수기
fine	adj. 괜찮은, 멋진, 화창한
accept	v. 받다, 수락하다, 수용하다
credit card	신용카드
certainly	adv. 물론(=of course, sure)
seat	n. 좌석, 자리
	v. 착석시키다, 앉히다
at least	적어도
prior to	~전에
departure	n. 출발
arrival	n. 도착
wonderful	adj. 멋진, 훌륭한
terrific	adj. 아주 멋진, 훌륭한, 무서운

Unit 4

see	v. 보다
passport	n. 여권
customs	n. 세관, 풍습
declaration form	신고서
embarkation card	출국 카드 (= departure card)
disembarkation card	입국 카드 (= arrival card)
declare	v. (세관이나 공항에서) 신고하다, 선언하다, 공표하다
purpose	n. 목적
nature	n. 성격, 자연, 본성, 성질

visit	n. 방문
	v. 방문하다
trip	n. 여행, 헛디딤
	v. (발이)걸리다, 헛디디다,
occupation	n. 직업, 종사, 점유, 점령
job	n. 일, 직업, 일자리
profession	n. 직업, 전문직
professor	n. 교수
be with + 학교, 회사	~학교나 회사에 근무하다
	(= work at ~, work for ~)
be going to	v. ~을 하려고하다, ~할 예정이다(= will)
sir	(손 윗 남자에 대한 경칭) 님, 씨, 아저씨
ma'am	(손 윗 여자에 대한 경칭) 마님, 아주머니, 님, 씨
reservation	n. 예약, (인디언) 보호 거주지
Just one moment	잠깐만요, 잠시만요
pay	v. 지불하다, 지급하다, 갚다
	n. 지불, 봉급, 보수
cash	n. 현금
	v. 현금으로 바꾸다
check-out time	퇴실시간
check-in time	입실시간
by noon	정오까지
sign	v. 서명하다, 사인하다, 날인하다
	n. 시호, 부호, 신호, 흔적, 징후
signature	n. 서명
bellman	n. (호텔 등의) 사환, 보이
baggage	n. 여행 짐가방, 수화물(= luggage)
enjoy	v. 즐기다, 향락하다, 누리다

Unit 6

Hello	int. 여보세요, 안녕하세요.
	n. 안부 예) Say hello to your mother.
available	adj. 이용할 수 있는, 소용이 되는
How many ~?	얼마나 많이 ~? (수를 나타낼 때)
party	n. 일행, 당파, 파티
Follow me.	저를 따라 오세요. = Come with me.
meal	n. 식사
coke	n. Coca-Cola의 약자
be ready to + 동사원형	~할 준비가 되다
try	v. 먹어보다, 써 보다, 입어보다, 해보다, 시도하다, 노력하다
	n. 시도, 해보기, 노력
eat	v. 먹다
taste	v. 맛보다, 시식하다
	n. 맛, 미각
never	adv. 일찍이 ~ 없다, 결코 ~않다
even	adv. ~까지도, ~조차도
once	n. 한 번
today's special	오늘의 특별요리
delicious	adj. 맛있는 (= tasty, good)
then	adv. 그렇다면, 그때에
cook	v. 요리하다
	n. 요리사

Unit 7

dressing	n. 소스, 드레싱 (= sauce)
tasteless	adj. 맛이 없는
bland	adj. 싱거운
terrible	adj. 형편없는
awful	adj. 끔직한, 형편없는, 지독한
dessert	n. 후식
desert	n. 사막
full	adj. 배부른, 가득 찬, 꽉 찬
satisfied	adj. 만족하는
check	n. 계산서(= bill), 수표, 저지, 검사, 점검 v. 조사하다, 확인하다, 저지하다, 억제하다, 점검하다, 대조하다
owe	v. 빚지고 있다, 은혜를 입고 있다
keep	v. 가지다, 유지하다, 보유하다, 지키다, 두다
take care of oneself	몸조심하다
take it easy	서두르지 마, 천천히 해

Unit 8

Excuse me!	실례합니다, 죄송합니다
need	v. 필요하다, 필요로 하다, ~할 필요가 있다 n. 필요, 궁핍
some	adj. 약간의, 얼마간의
directions	n. 길 안내, 방향, 지시, 지도
do sightseeing	관광을 하다
tourist attractions	관광명소
famous	adj. 유명한
tourist places	관광지
What's so good about~?	~이 뭐가 그렇게 좋습니까?
tall	adj. 높은, 키가 큰
high	adj. 높은
spectacular	adj. 장관의, 볼만한
breathtaking	adj. 아슬아슬한, 숨 막히는, 굉장한
view	n. 광경, 경치, 전망, 구경, 조망, 목적, 견해
impressive	adj. 인상적인
thrillingly	adv. 스릴 있게, 짜릿하게, 오싹하게,
feel like + ing	~을 하고 싶어 하다, ~하고 싶은 느낌이 들다
direct	가리키다, 지시하다, 지도하다
just around the corner	바로 코너 모퉁이에
miss	v. 놓치다, ~를 그리워하다
find	v. 찾다, 발견하다
easily	adv. 쉽게, 용이하게

traffic jam	교통 혼잡, 교통 체증(= heavy traffic)
nearest	adj. 가장 가까운 (= closest)
withdraw	v. 인출하다, 빼다, 물러나다, 철회하다,
deposit	v. 예금하다, 맡기다, 집어넣다
	n. 예금, 맡김, 기탁, 공탁금
ATM	자동 예금 인출기

Unit 9

rent	v. 대여하다, 임대하다, 빌리다
	n. 집세, 임대
What kind of ~?	어떤 종류의 ~?
back seat	뒷좌석
front seat	앞좌석
recommend	v. 추천하다, 권하다, 권고하다
enjoyable	adj. 즐거운, 재미있는, 유쾌한
ride	n. 탐, 태움
	v. (말, 자전거, 차량) 등을 타다
suggest	v. 제의(제안)하다, 암시하다, 시사 하다
comfortable	adj. 편안한, 안락한
uncomfortable	adj. 불편한
rate	n. 요금, 비율, 등급
	v. 평가하다, 어림잡다
a day	하루에 (= per day)
without	prep. ~없이, 포함하지 않고

driver's license	운전 면허증
right here	바로 여기
mileage	n. 마일리지, 기름 사용량
gas(oline)	n. 휘발유, 가솔린
charge	n. 청구 금액, 대가, 요금, 장전, 충천, 비난, 고소, 돌격 v. 요금을 청구하다, 충전하다, (신용카드)에 대금을 달다, 값을 달다, 돌격하다
fill up	가득 채우다
bring back	가져오다, 반환하다, 돌아오다
midnight	n. 자정, 밤 12시

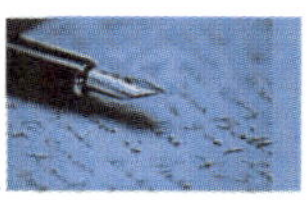

Unit 10

get	v. 가지다, 사다
ring	n. 반지 v. (방울, 종, 전화기 등이) 울리다
husband	n. 남편
spend	v. 소비하다, 쓰다
budget	n. 예산, 경비, 운영비
around	adv. 대략, 대충, 약 (= about, approximately)
karat	n. 캐럿
regular price	정가
additional	adj. 추가적인, 추가의

discount	n. 할인, 디스카운트 할인하다, 가격을 깎아 주다
otherwise	adv. 그렇지 않으면
might have to ~	~해야만 한다
shop around	~ 여기 저기 돌아다니다
bottom price	최저 가격, 바닥 가격
guarantee	v. 보증하다, 확언한다, 장담하다 n. 보증,개런티(최저 보증 출연료)
lowest	adj. 최저의, 가장 저렴한
besides	adv. 게다가, 또한, 더욱이 (= moreover, in addition)
don't have to	~할 필요가 없다
sales tax	판매세
wrap	v. 포장하다, 감다, (감)싸다, 접다

APPENDIX 1

오10일투자,

냉(가슴)뻥(뚫린)영어

부록1 • APPENDIX

1. 인칭대명사의 격변화

인칭	격	주격		소유격	목적격	소유 대명사	재귀 대명사
	수	~은, ~이, ~가		~의	~을, ~에게	~의 것	~자신
1인칭			be동사				
	단수	I	am	my	me	mine	myself
	복수	we	are	our	us	ours	ourselves
2인칭	단수	you	are	your	you	yours	yourself
	복수	you	are	your	you	yours	yourselves
3인칭	단수	he	is	his	him	his	himself
		she	is	her	her	hers	herself
		it	is	its	it	(its)	itself
	복수	they	are	their	them	theirs	themselves

2. 불규칙동사의 변화

원형 · 과거형 · 과거 분사형 모두 동일한 형태(A-A-A Type)

내기하다	bet	bet	bet
비용이 들다	cost	cost	cost
자르다	cut	cut	cut
때리다	hit	hit	hit
다치게 하다	hurt	hurt	hurt
시키다	let	let	let
두다	put	put	put
그만두다	quit	quit	quit
읽다	read	read	read
닫다	shut	shut	shut
쪼개다	split	split	split
펴지다	spread	spread	spread

과거형 · 과거분사형이 동일한 형태(A-B-B Type)

가져오다	bring	brought	brought
사다	buy	bought	bought
잡다	catch	caught	caught
싸우다	fight	fought	fought
구하다	seek	sought	sought

• 가르치다	teach	taught	taught
• 생각하다	think	thought	thought
• 구부리다	bend	bent	bent
• 빌려 주다	lend	lent	lent
• 보내다	send	sent	sent
• 쓰다	spend	spent	spent
• 세우다	build	built	built
• 이기다	win	won	won
• 찾다	find	found	found
• 감다	wind	wound	wound
• 파다	dig	dug	dug
• 매달다	hang	hung	hung
• 돌리다	spin	spun	spun
• 달라붙다	stick	stuck	stuck
• 치다	strike	struck	struck
• 흔들리다	swing	swung	swung
• 듣다	hear	heard	heard
• 잡다	hold	held	held
• 잃다	lose	lost	lost
• 팔다	sell	sold	sold
• 말하다	tell	told	told
• 빛나다	shine	shone	shone
• 서다	stand	stood	stood
• 이해하다	understand	understood	understood
• 피나다	bleed	bled	bled

먹이다	feed	fed	fed
오해하다	misunderstand	misunderstood	misunderstood
도망가다	flee	fled	fled
이끌다	lead	led	led
속력 내다	speed	sped	sped
다루다	deal	dealt	dealt
느끼다	feel	felt	felt
보관하다	keep	kept	kept
떠나다	leave	left	left
의미하다	mean	meant	meant
잠자다	sleep	slept	slept
만나다	meet	met	met
앉다	sit	sat	sat
쏘다	shoot	shot	shot
지불하다	pay	paid	paid
말하다	say	said	said
가지다	have	had	had
만들다	make	made	made

원형 · 과거형 · 과거분사형이 서로 다른 형태(A-B-C Type)

시작하다	begin	began	begun
하다	do	did	done
마시다	drink	drank	drunk
날다	fly	flew	flown

울리다	ring	rang	rung
노래하다	sing	sang	sung
줄어들다	shrink	shrank	shrunk
침몰하다	sink	sank	sunk
수영하다	swim	swam	swum
낳다	bear	bore	born
물다	bite	bit	bitten
깨다	break	broke	broken
고르다	choose	chose	chosen
얼다	freeze	froze	frozen
숨다	hide	hid	hidden
눕다	lie	lay	lain
말하다	speak	spoke	spoken
훔치다	steal	stole	stolen
맹세하다	swear	swore	sworn
찢다	tear	tore	torn
입다	wear	wore	worn
깨다	wake	woke	woken
이다	am, is(are)	was(were)	been
때리다	beat	beat	beaten
불다	blow	blew	blown
그리다	draw	drew	drawn
운전하다	drive	drove	driven
먹다	eat	ate	eaten
떨어지다	fall	fell	fallen

• 자라다	grow	grew	grown
• 알다	know	knew	known
• 타다	ride	rode	ridden
• 가다	go	went	gone
• 오르다	rise	rose	risen
• 보다	see	saw	seen
• 흔들다	shake	shook	shaken
• 면도하다	shave	shaved	shaven
• 보여 주다	show	showed	shown
• 부어 오르다	swell	swelled	swollen
• 용서하다	forgive	forgave	forgiven
• 주다	give	gave	given
• 가지다	take	took	taken
• 잊다	forget	forgot	forgotten
• 얻다	get	got	got(gotten)
• 실수하다	mistake	mistook	mistaken
• 던지다	throw	threw	thrown
• 쓰다	write	wrote	written

원형과 과거분사형이 같은 형태(A-B-A Type)

• 되다	become	became	become
• 오다	come	came	come
• 달리다	run	ran	run

조동사의 불규칙변화

할 수 있다	can	could	-
해도 된다	may	might	-
할 것이다	will	would	-
해야만 한다	must	must	-
해야 한다	shall	should	-

3. 규칙동사의 변화

t발음 : t 이외의 무성음(p. k. f, θ, s, ʃ, tʃ)으로 끝나는 동사 다음

burp	clip	drop	help	stop	type
wipe	ask	bake	cook	kick	knock
look	pack	park	pick	shock	talk
walk	work	cough	laugh		
cross	dance	dress	embarrass	fix	kiss
miss	mix	brush	finish	wash	wish
pitch	punch	watch			

d 발음: d 이외의 유성음(모음과 b, d, g, v, z, m, n, l, w, j, r 등) 다음

- allow arrive bury clean climb comb
- compose cry dial die dry dye
- fail kill lay lie listen live
- love mail marry measure move play
- pour prove rain return sail seize
- shave show smile snow study tour
- try turn vacuum worry yawn

id 발음: 어미가 d와 t 발음으로 끝나는 동사 다음

- act aid calculate complicate concentrate
- date defeat depart desert disappoint
- dust excite exhibit expect frustrate
- hate hint imitate immigrate interest
- incite paint paste plant print
- repeat rest shout start submit
- succeed sweat

4. 대학전공 과목명

- Anatomy 해부학
- Anthropology 인류학
- Architecture 건축학
- Astronomy 천문학
- Biochemistry 생화학
- Botany 식물학
- Chemistry 화학
- Civil Engineering 토목공학
- Computer Science 컴퓨터공학
- Criminology 범죄학
- Dentistry 치과의학
- East Asian Studies 동양학
- Economics 경제학
- Education 교육학
- Electrical Engineering 전기공학
- English 영어학
- English Language and Literature 영어영문학
- English Literature 영문학
- Environmental Engineering 환경공학
- Forestry 임학
- French Language and Literature 불어불문학

- Geography 지리학
- Geology 지질학
- History 역사학
- Industrial Engineering 생산관리공학
- International Relations 국제관계학
- Law 법학
- Linguistics and Information Science 문헌정보학
- Linguistics 언어학
- Management 경영학
- Mathematics 수학
- Mechanical Engineering 기계공학
- Microbiology 미생물학
- Music 음악학
- Nutritional Science 식품영양학
- Pharmacy 약학
- Philosophy 철학
- Physics 물리학
- Physiology 생리학
- Political Science 정치학
- Psychology 심리학
- Religious Studies 종교학
- Sociology 사회학
- Statistics 통계학
- Zoology 동물학

5. 시사영어 약자(abbreviations)

- AIDS Acquired Immune Deficiency Syndrome (후천성 면역결핍증)
- APEC Asia-Pacific Economic Cooperation (아태경제 협력체)
- ASEM Asia-Europe Meeting (아시아유럽정상회담)
- ASEAN Association of Southeast Asian Nations (동남아연합)
- CIA Central Intelligence Agency (미 중앙정보국)
- CIS Commonwealth of Independent States (독립국가연합)
- DMZ Demilitarized Zone (비무장 지대)
- EEZ Exclusive Economic Zone (배타적 경제수역)
- EU European Union (유럽연합)
- FBI Federal Bureau of Investigation (미 연방수사국)
- G8 Group of Eight (the U.S., England, Germany, France, Japan, Italy, Canada, Russia)
- GATT General Agreement on Tariffs and Trade (관세 및 무역에 관한 일반협정)
- GDP Gross Domestic Product (국내총생산)
- GNP Gross National Product (국민총생산)
- HDTV High Definition TV (고화질 TV)
- IAEA International Atomic Energy Agency (국제원자력기구)
- IBM International Business Machines Corporation

- IBRD International Bank for Reconstruction and Development (국제부흥개발은행)
- ILO International Labor Organization (국제노동기구)
- IMF International Monetary Fund (국제통화기금)
- Interpol International Criminal Police Organization (국제경찰)
- KEDO Korean Peninsula Energy Development Organization (한반도 에너지 개발기구)
- NAFTA North American Free Trade Agreement (북미자유무역협정)
- NASA National Aeronautics Space Adminstration (미항공우주국)
- NATO North Atlantic Treaty Organization (북대서양조약기구)
- NICS Newly Industrialized Countries (신흥공업국)
- NIMBY Not In My Back Yard (님비사상)
- NPT Nuclear Non-Proliferation Treaty (핵확산방지조약)
- OECD Organization for Economic Cooperation and Development (경제협력개발기구)
- OEM Original Equipment Manufacturing (주문자상표부착판매)
- OPEC Organization of the Petroleum Exporting Countries (석유수출국)
- PIMFY Please In My Front Yard (핌피사상)
- PKO Peace Keeping Operations (of the UN) (유엔평화유지활동)
- ROK Republic of Korea (대한민국)

- SOC Social Overhead Capital (사회간접자본)
- SDI Strategic Defense Initiative (전략방어구상)
- SOFA Status of Forces Agreement (한미행정협정)
- UNESCO United Nations Educational, Scientific, and Cultural Organization (유엔교육과학문화기구)
- UN United Nations (국제연합)
- UNICEF United Nations International Children's Emergency Fund(유엔 아동기금)
- VAT Value Added Tax (부가가치세)
- WHO World Health Organizations (세계보건기구)
- WTO World Trade Organization (국제무역기구)
- WTO World Tourism Organization(세계관광기구)
- Hot line 직통전화선
- Achilles' heel 아킬레스 건, 치명적인 약점
- hot potato 뜨거운 감자, 미묘한 문제
- lame duck 레임덕, 권력누수현상

6. 서양의 황도십이궁

- Aries(Ram) 21th March-19th April
  양자리(백양궁)
- Taurus(Bull) 20th April-21st May
  황소자리(금우궁)

- Gemini(Twins) 22nd May-20th June
  쌍둥이자리(쌍자궁)
- Cancer(Crab) 21st June-22nd July
  게자리(거해궁)
- Leo(Lion) 23rd July-22nd August
  사자자리(사자궁)
- Virgo(Virgin) 23rd August-22nd September
  처녀자리(처녀궁)
- Libra(Balance) 23rd September-22nd October
  천칭자리(천칭궁)
- Scorpio(Scorpion) 23rd October-21st November
  전갈자리(천갈궁)
- Sagittarius(Archer) 22nd November-21st December
  궁수자리(인마궁)
- Capricorn(Goat) 22nd December-19th January
  염소자리(마갈궁)
- Aquarius(Water-bearer) 20th January-19th February
  물병자리(보병궁)
- Pisces(Fishes) 20th February-20th March
  물고기자리(쌍어궁)

7. 동양의 십이지

Rat	子	쥐
Ox	丑	소
Tiger	寅	호랑이
Hare	卯	토끼
Dragon	辰	용
Serpent	巳	뱀
Horse	午	말
Sheep	未	양
Monkey	申	원숭이
Hen	酉	닭
Dog	戌	개
Pig	亥	돼지

8. 기수와 서수 읽기

기수 (Cardinal Numbers)

1	one	2	two
3	three	4	four
5	five	6	six
7	seven	8	eight

9	nine	10	ten
11	eleven	12	twelve
13	thirteen	14	fourteen
15	fifteen	16	sixteen
17	seventeen	18	eighteen
19	nineteen	20	twenty
21	twenty-one	…………	
29	twenty-nine	30	thirty
40	forty	50	fifty
60	sixty	70	seventy
80	eighty	90	ninety
100	one hundred	1,000	one thousand

- 10,000 ten thousand
- 100,000 one hundred thousand
- 1,000,000 one million
- 10,000,000 ten million

서수 (Original Numbers)

1st	first	2nd	second
3rd	third	4th	fourth
5th	fifth	6th	sixth
7th	seventh	8th	eighth
9th	ninth	10th	tenth
11th	eleventh	12th	twelfth

13th	thirteenth	14th	fourteenth
15th	fifteenth	16th	sixteenth
17th	seventeenth	18th	eighteenth
19th	nineteenth	20th	twentieth
21th	twenty-first	············	
29th	twenty-ninth	30th	thirtieth
31th	thirty-first	40th	fortieth
41th	forty-first	50th	fiftieth
51th	fifty-first	60th	sixtieth
70th	seventieth	80th	eightieth
90th	ninetieth	100th	one hundredth
1,000th	one thousandth		

APPENDIX 2
꼭! 알아둡시다

오10일투자,

냉(가슴)뻥(뚫린)영어

꼭! 알아둡시다

방향

- 동(쪽) east(eastern 동쪽의)
- 서(쪽) west(western 서쪽의)
- 남(쪽) south(southern 남쪽의)
- 북(쪽) north(northern 북쪽의)

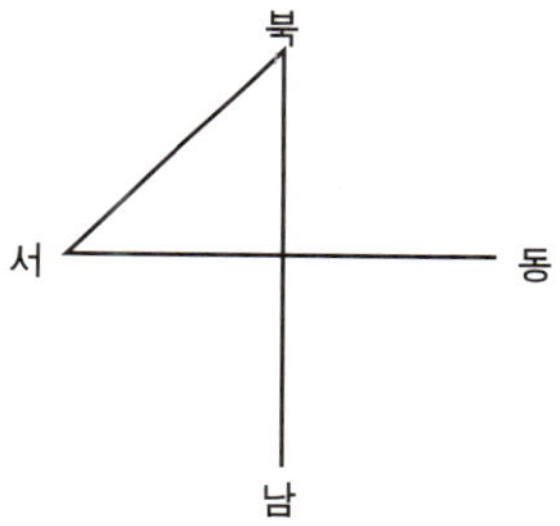

미국대학의 학년 명

- freshman 1학년
- sophomore 2학년
- junior 3학년
- senior 4학년

신체부위명

- head 머리
- eye 눈
- face 얼굴
- ear 귀

- nose 코
- stomach 위
- mouth 입
- chest 가슴
- arm 팔
- forearm 팔뚝
- hand 손
- leg 다리
- knee 무릎
- abdomen 배
- neck 목
- shoulder 어깨
- waist 허리
- palm 손바닥
- ankle 발목
- tongue 혀
- forehead 이마
- lung 허파
- heart 심장
- pupil 눈동자(동공)
- beard 턱수염
- eyelash 속눈썹
- mustache 콧수염
- finger 손가락
- lip 입술
- chin 턱
- hair 머리카락
- wrist 손목
- thumb 엄지손가락
- finger nail 손톱
- thigh 허벅지
- foot 발
- toe 발가락
- back 등
- elbow 팔꿈치
- hip 엉덩이
- calf 장딴지
- heel 발꿈치
- brain 뇌
- throat 목구멍
- eyebrow 눈썹
- cheek 볼
- tooth 이
- liver 간
- eyelid 눈거풀

가족관계

- grand parents 조부모님
- grandfather 할아버지
- grandmother 할머니
- parents 부모님
- father 아버지
- mother 어머니
- father-in-law 장인, 시아버지
- mother-in-law 장모, 시어머니
- children 자녀
- son 아들
- daughter 딸
- son-in-law 사위
- daughter-in-law 며느리
- brother 형제
- elder(older) brother 형
- younger brother 남동생
- elder(older) sister 언니
- younger sister 여동생
- sister 자매
- brother-in-law 매형, 매제
- sister-in-law 형수, 올케
- uncle (외)삼촌
- aunt (외)숙모
- nephew 조카
- niece 질녀
- cousin (외)사촌
- grand children 손주
- grandson 손자
- granddaughter 손녀

일주일년

- day 일
- week 주
- month 월
- year 년

요일

- Sunday 일
- Monday 월
- Tuesday 화
- Wednesday 수
- Thursday 목
- Friday 금
- Saturday 토

월

- January 1월
- February 2월
- March 3월
- April 4월
- May 5월
- June 6월
- July 7월
- August 8월
- September 9월
- October 10월
- November 11월
- December 12월

사계절

- spring 봄
- summer 여름
- fall 또는 autumn 가을
- winter 겨울

하루의 시점

- morning 아침
- afternoon 오후
- night 밤
- noon 정오
- evening 저녁
- midnight 자정

시점의 분류

- the day before yesterday 그저께
- yesterday 어제
- today 오늘
- tomorrow 내일
- the day after tomorrow 모레
- yesterday morning 어제 아침
- yesterday afternoon 어제 오후
- yesterday evening 어제 저녁
- last night 어젯밤
- this morning 오늘 아침
- this afternoon 오늘 오후
- this evening 오늘 저녁
- tonight 오늘밤
- tomorrow night 내일밤

식사 명

- breakfast 아침
- lunch 점심
- dinner 저녁
- supper 저녁
- brunch 아침 겸 점심
- snack 간식

방향과 장소의 전치사 및 부사

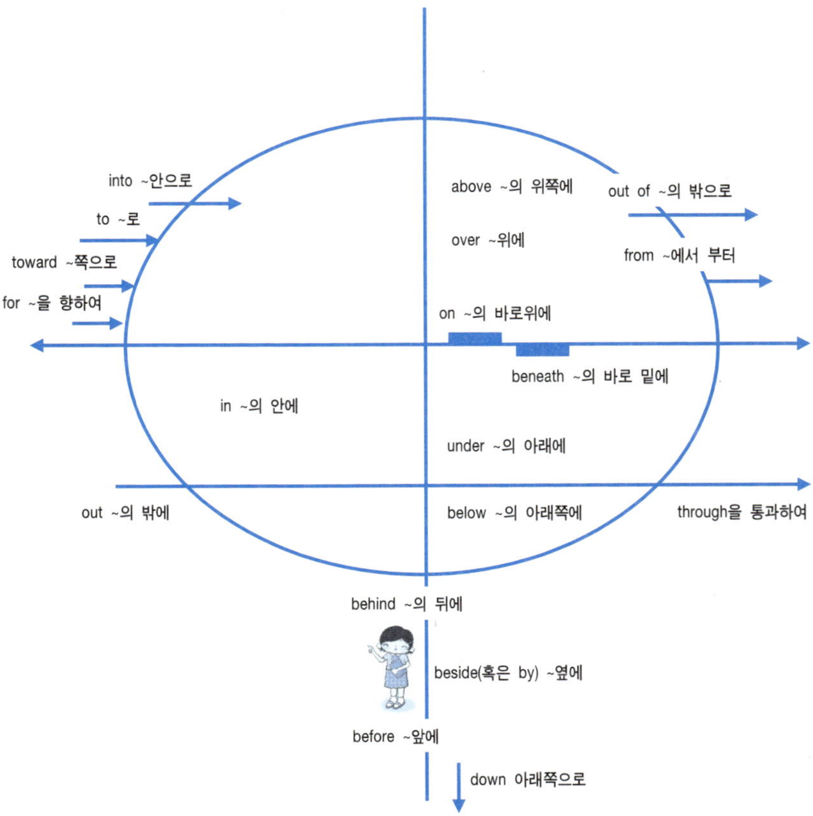

- into ~안으로
- toward ~쪽으로
- in ~의 안에
- up 위쪽으로
- over ~의 위에
- out of ~의 밖으로
- in ~의 안에
- beneath ~의 바로 밑에
- below ~의 아래쪽에
- behind ~의 뒤에
- before ~앞에
- to ~로
- for ~을 향하여
- out ~의 밖에
- above ~의 위쪽에
- on ~의 바로 위에
- from ~에서 부터
- out ~의 밖에
- under ~의 아래에
- through을 통과하여
- beside(혹은 by) ~옆에
- down 아래쪽으로

태양 둘레를 타원궤도로 공전하는 9개의 천체

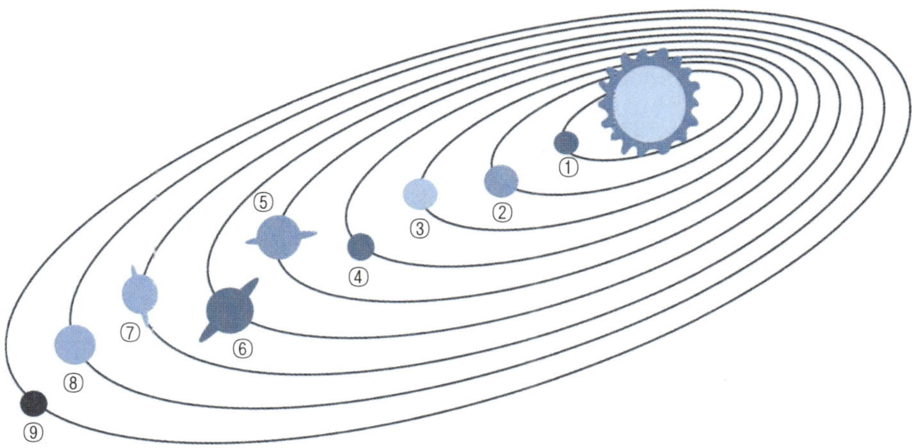

- ① Mercury 수성
- ② Venus 금성
- ③ Earth 지구
- ④ Mars 화성
- ⑤ Jupiter 목성
- ⑥ Saturn 토성
- ⑦ Uranus 천왕성
- ⑧ Neptune 해왕성
- ⑨ Pluto 명왕성

동물이름

- bat 박쥐
- bear 곰
- camel 낙타
- cat 고양이
- cow 소
- crocodile 악어
- deer 사슴
- dog 개
- donkey 나귀
- elephant 코끼리
- fox 여우
- frog 개구리
- giraffe 기린
- goat 염소
- gorilla 고릴라
- leopard 표범
- hippopotamus 하마
- horse 말
- kangaroo 캥거루
- koala 코알라
- lion 사자
- lizard 도마뱀
- monkey 원숭이
- mouse 쥐
- polar bear 북극(흰)곰
- panda 팬다곰
- pig 돼지
- puppy 강아지
- rabbit 토끼
- reindeer 순록
- sheep 양
- snail 달팽이

- snake 뱀
- spider 거미
- squirrel 다람쥐
- tiger 호랑이
- wolf 늑대
- zebra 얼룩말

스포츠 게임

- baseball 야구

- tennis 테니스

- soccer 축구

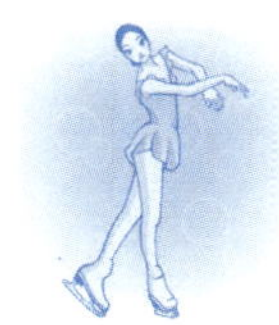

- figure skating 피겨 스케이팅

- basketball 농구

- ice hockey 아이스하키

- rugby 럭비

- table tennis 탁구

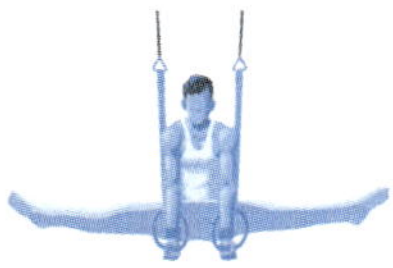

- gymnastics 체조

- skiing 스키

- wrestling 레슬링

- boxing 복싱

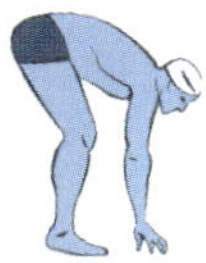

- swimming 수영

- horse racing 승마경주

- running 육상

- cycling 사이클링

- squash 스쿼시

- mountain climing 등산

- football 미식축구

- volleyball 배구

가벼운 병명

- headache 두통
- backache 요통
- stomachache 위통(복통)
- influenza(=flu) 독감
- diarrhea 설사
- sea sickness 배 멀미
- air sickness 비행기 멀미
- toothache 치통
- earache 귀앓이
- cold 감기
- fever 열
- morning sickness 입덧
- car sickness 차 멀리

성 앞에 흔히 쓰이는 약자

- Dr. 의사, 박사(=doctor)
- Mr. (남성의 성. 이름 앞에 붙이는 경칭어) ~씨, ~군(=mister)
- Mrs. (기혼 부인의 남편의 성 앞에 붙이는 경칭어) ~부인, ~씨, 마님
- Miss (미혼여성에 대한 경칭어) ~양, ~아가씨
- Ms. (여성의 미혼, 기혼여부를 모를때 성, 이름 앞에 붙이는 경칭어)

빈도부사

- never 결코(0%)
- rarely 드물게(10%)
- sometimes 가끔씩(50%)
- often 종종(70%)
- usually 보통(90%)
- always 항상(100%)

미국, 캐나다 돈의 동전단위

- penny 1 cent
- nickel 5 cents
- dime 10cents
- quarter 25 cents

옷 사이즈

- small 소
- medium 중
- large 대
- exrta large 특대

과일종류

- apple 사과
- melon 참외
- strawberry 딸기
- orange 귤
- coconut 코코넛
- mango 망고
- tomato 토마토
- cherry 앵두
- chestnut 밤
- peanut 땅콩
- lemon 레몬
- peach 복숭아
- watermelon 수박
- plum 자두
- cantaloupe 캔탈로프
- pineapple 파인애플
- grape 포도
- banana 바나나
- pear 배
- walnut 호도
- apricot 살구
- grapefruit 그레이프프루트

의문문의 6하원칙

- who 누가, 누구
- where 어디(서)
- why 왜
- when 언제
- what 무엇(을)
- how 어떻게

복합관계 부사

- whoever 누구든지
- wherever 어디든지
- however 어떻게든지
- whenever 언제든지
- whatever 무엇이든지

색깔

- red 빨
- yellow 노
- blue 파
- violet 보
- black 검정
- pink 핑크
- gold 금
- purple 자주
- orange 주
- green 초
- indigo 남
- white 흰
- silver 은
- gray 회
- brown 갈
- sky blue 하늘

보석류

- gold 금
- ruby 루비
- silver 은
- pearl 진주

- sapphire 사파이어
- topaz 황수정
- emerald 에메랄드
- diamond 다이아몬드

액세서리

- earring 귀걸이
- watch 시계
- tie clip 넥타이 클립
- necklace 목걸이
- bracelet 팔찌
- cuff link 커프링크
- ring 반지

10일투자

냉(가슴) 뻥(뚫린) 영어 **(Audio CD 포함)**

2009년 12월 24일 초판 1쇄 인쇄
2009년 12월 30일 초판 1쇄 발행

공저자 문 귀 남·박 양 우
발행인 (寅製) 진 욱 상

발행처 백산출판사
서울시 성북구 정릉3동 653-40
등록 : 1974. 1. 9. 제 1-72호
전화 : 914-1621, 917-6240
FAX : 912-4438
http://www.ibaeksan.kr
edit@ibaeksan.kr
biz@ibaeksan.kr

값 10,000원
ISBN 978-89-6183-248-9